Drawing With Letters

The HAUNTED CREEPS AND GHASTLY GHOULS of SPIDERBITE

STEVE HARPSTER

D1444913

HARPTOONS™ PUBLISHING

WWW.HARPTOONS.COM

This book is dedicated to my son, Tyler.
Keep being your awesome self!

www.harptoons.com

Library of Congress Cataloging-in-Publication Data
Library of Congress Control Number: 2012916155
Harpster, Steve
Drawing With Letters; The Haunted Creeps and Ghastly Ghouls of Spiderbite- written and illustrated by Steve Harpster

SUMMARY: Learn how to draw 26 scary characters of the Spiderbite house using letters. ART / General, JUVENILE FICTION / General

ISBN: 0-615-68599-4
ISBN: 978-0-615-68599-1
SAN: 859-6921

Printed in the United States of America by Bookmasters, Inc. 30 Amberwood Parkway, Ashland, OH 44805 JOB # M9998   Date of production - 9/6/12

Beware of Spiderbite House, for inside lurks the odd and unexplained. Ghosts float through the walls, while creatures of the night hide in darkness. There's no telling what you will find in this house of haunts. So enter if you dare, and behold the freaky frights of Spiderbite!

Anthony resides in the swamp at Spiderbite. No one knows how he came to this swamp, but rumors say he has an older brother at Loch Ness.

Bitey is the Spiderbite guard dog. This sharp-toothed hound has a bite far worse than its bark.

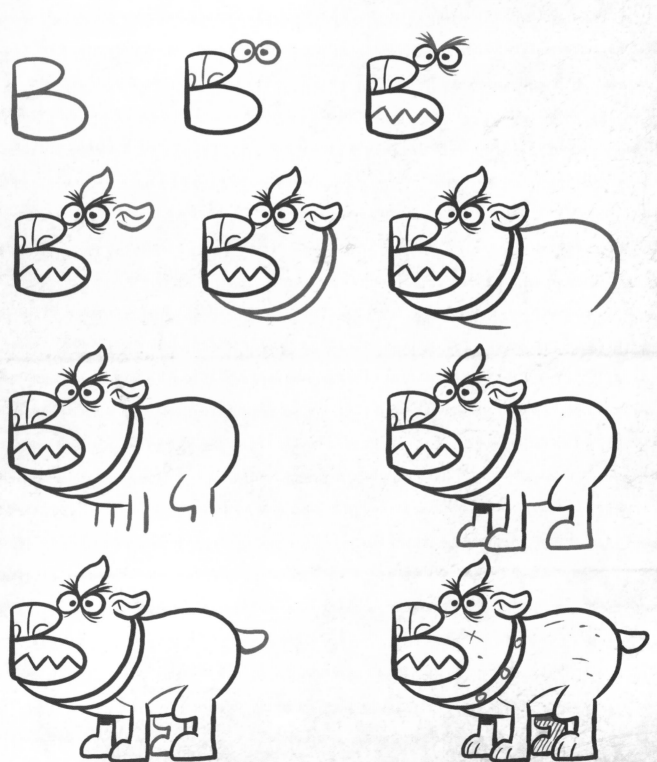

Crash is just one of the many ghosts of Spiderbite.
He suffers from a severe case of narcolepsy and
has a terrible disposition. As long as Crash doesn't
sleep, no one else will either.

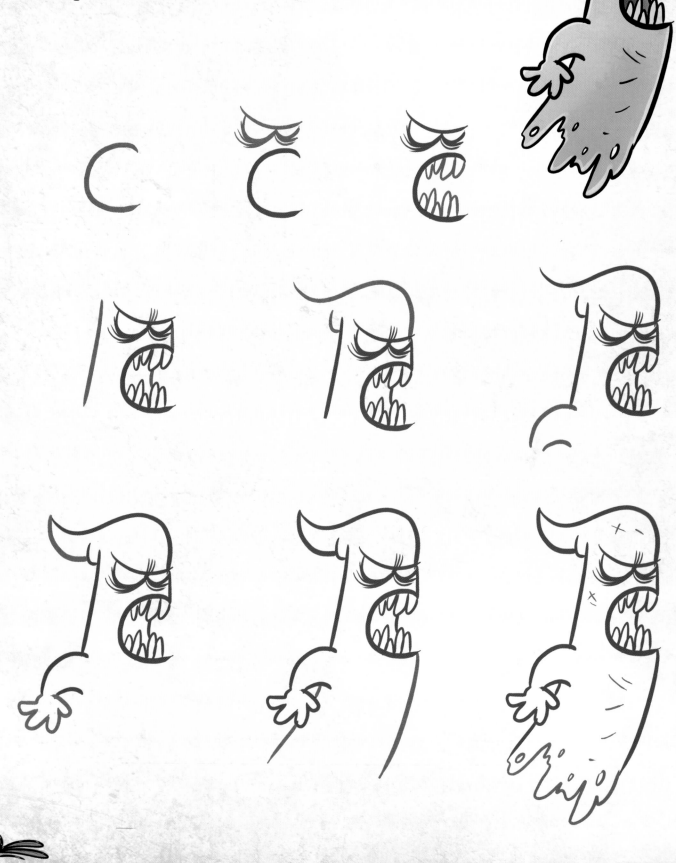

Dave also calls Spiderbite swamp his home. He sings like a frog, swims like a fish, and eats like a crocodile.

Eddie Ecto Goo is pure slime. He can change shape, stick to the walls, and ooze through almost any crack or opening.

Draw Eddie Ecto Goo in different shapes and poses. His gooey body can do almost anything.

Freddy Bones is a real joker and loves pulling pranks. Scaring the daylights out of the living really tickles Freddy's funny bone.

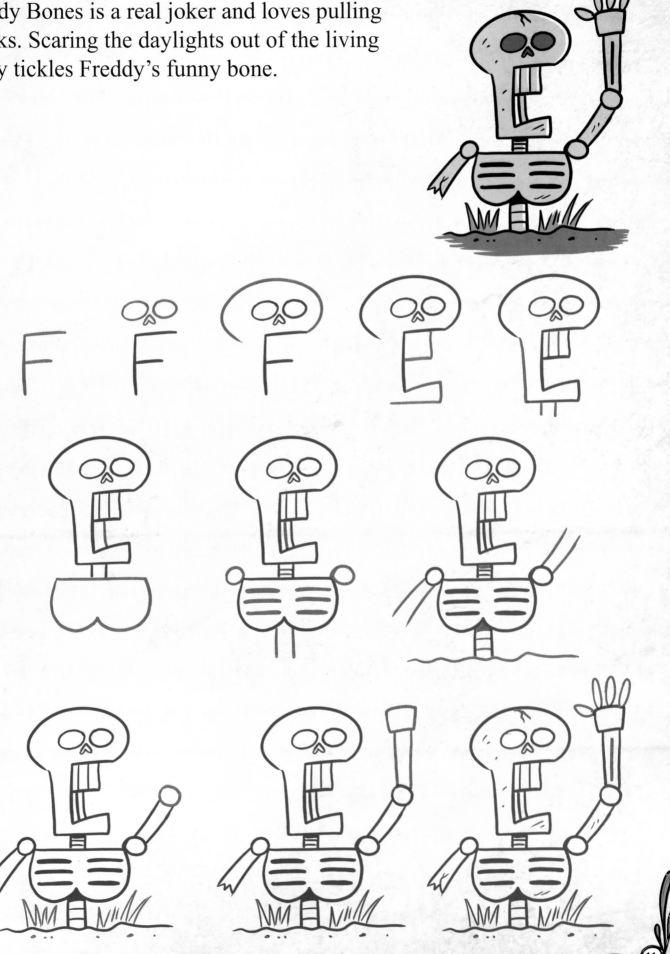

Gunk works at Spiderbite as the house cook. He makes a wonderful squid eye pie and a to-die-for bat fang soup. Try them if you dare.

Hank is the chauffeur of the motor car for Dr. Tinkoor. He is an excellent driver and never makes a wrong turn or goes over the speed limit--at least, no one has ever had the guts to tell him.

Igg was once an iguana until the mad scientist, Dr. Tinkoor, turned him into a monster. Igg roams the grounds looking for his next meal, but don't worry, he's a vegetarian.

Jasper, the old vulture, is a long time resident of Spiderbite. His favorite food is anything dead and the longer it's been dead the better.

Killer man-eating plants live around the grounds of Spiderbite. These plants have never actually eaten a man and it's doubtful that they could, but who is going to get close enough to find out?

Lady Lenor runs Spiderbite House. Nothing is done without her permission. She has a wicked gaze and bad temper, but under all that scariness is a heart of gold.

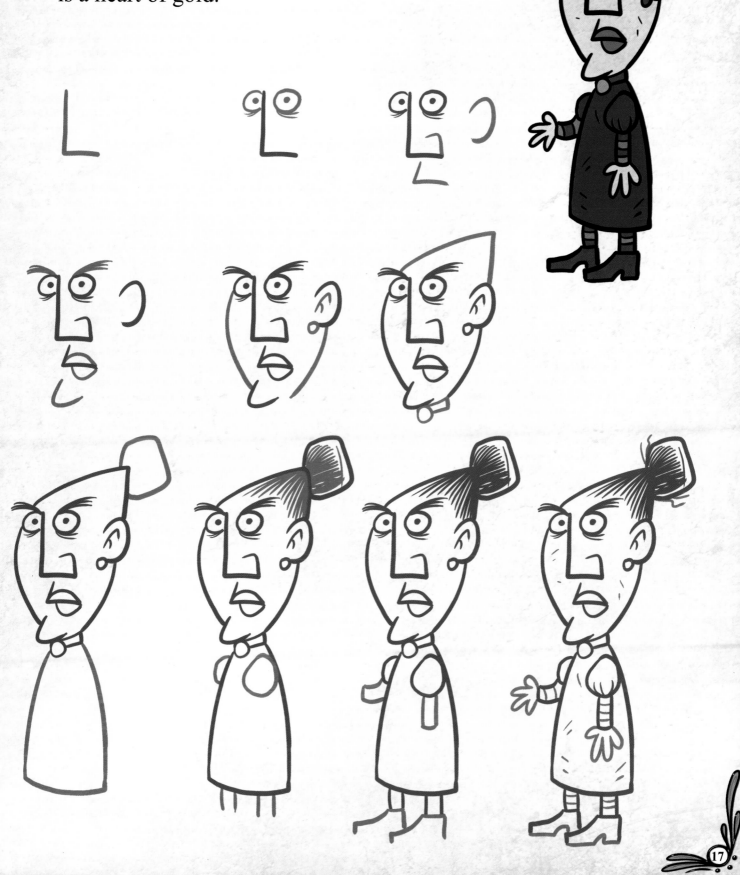

Mortimer is the butler of Spiderbite. He answers the door and the phone without saying a word. Unfortunately for poor Mortimer, he doesn't have a tongue.

Nasty bats live in the attics and rafters of Spiderbite. They fly around at night in search of food, squeaking and flapping with delight.

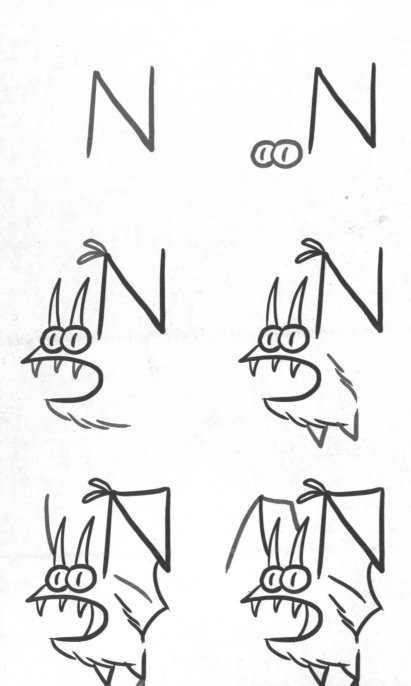

Oliver is Lady Lenor's only son, and the youthful spirit of Spiderbite. He loves playing games like *Chutes and Coffins* or *Hungry Hungry Eels*. He also spends time on the web looking for big hairy spiders.

Wolfy was the family pet until he was turned into a monster, or was he a monster turned into the family pet?

Quinton spends his days hanging around.
Then when nightfall comes, Quinton lurks
around looking for trouble. This wiry man of
straw can scare more than just crows away.

Rats of Spiderbite are truly unique. These rats are very smart and live in what looks like a "rat city" inside the walls of the Spiderbite home.

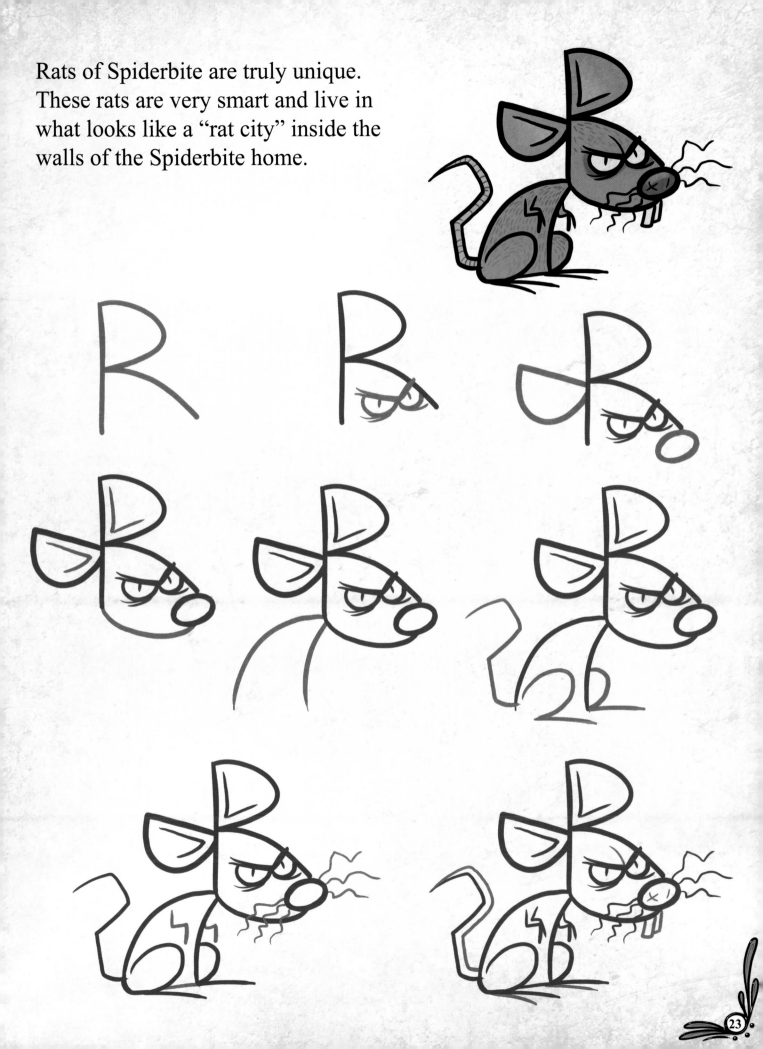

Skugs are odd little bugs found all over
Spiderbite. They are so incredibly smart
that they might not be bugs at all but very
tiny aliens from another planet.

Dr. Tinkoor is a mad scientist and owner of Spiderbite. His experiments are strange, his creations are odd. He has been banned by the medical community, the scientific community, and the home owners association.

The griffin is a truly remarkable beast. At Spiderbite it's hard to know: is this a mythological creature come to life or just another strange creation of Dr. Tinkoor?

Victor the owl watches with his bright glowing eyes. Occasionally he lets out a sharp "who" but never a "why."

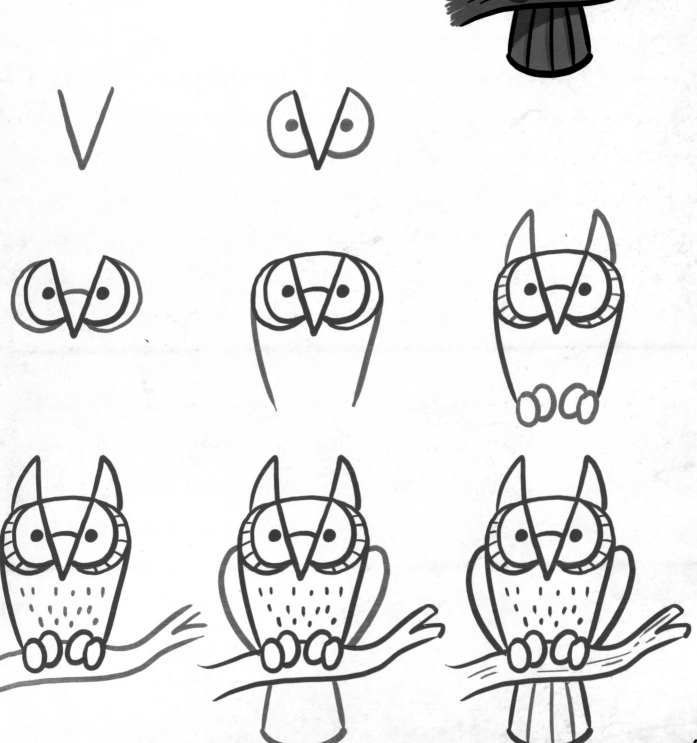

Watching gargoyles stand guard and protect Spiderbite. They are made of stone, but people swear they come to life and even fly.

Many of the trees at Spiderbite seem to stare with big glowing eyes--keeping a close watch and reporting on any tresspassers.

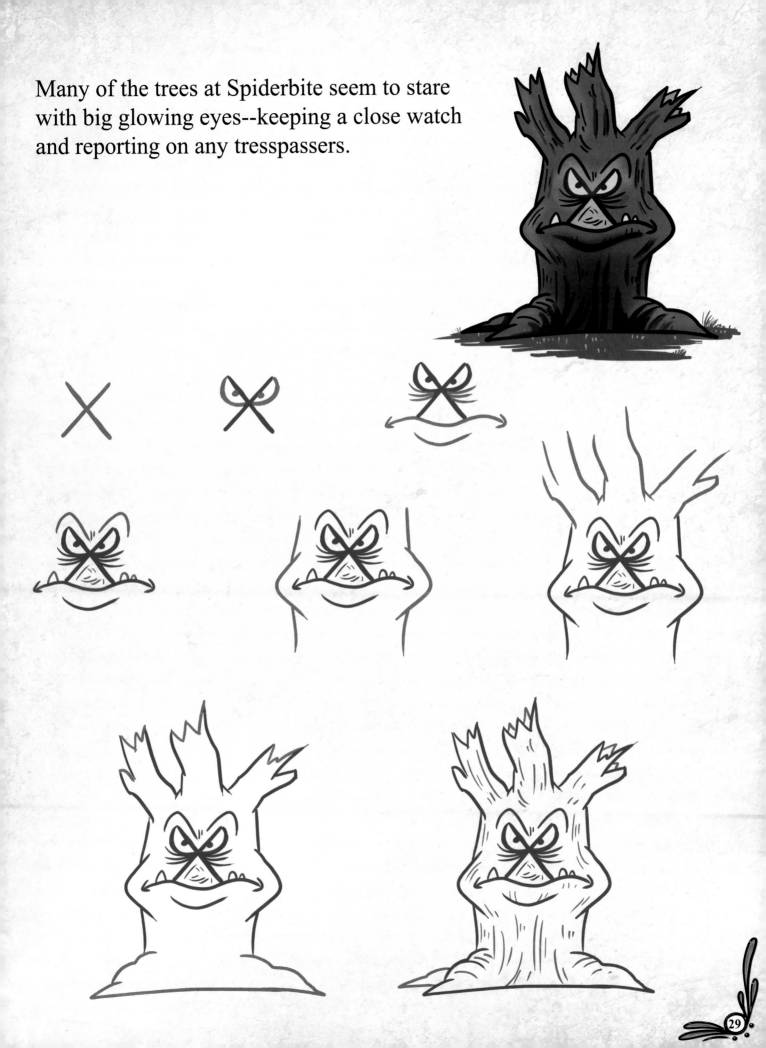

Yugg used all nine of his lives a long time ago. He was brought back to life by Dr. Tinkoor, and now roams the halls of Spiderbite, never eating or sleeping.

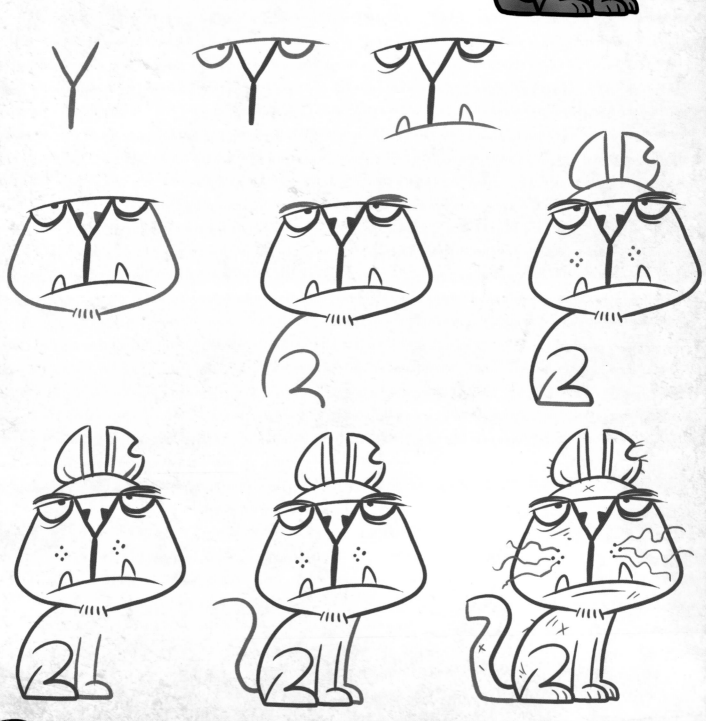

Zip is Lady Lenor's most beloved pet. Just look at those cute beady eyes and sharp poisonous fangs. Who wouldn't love him?

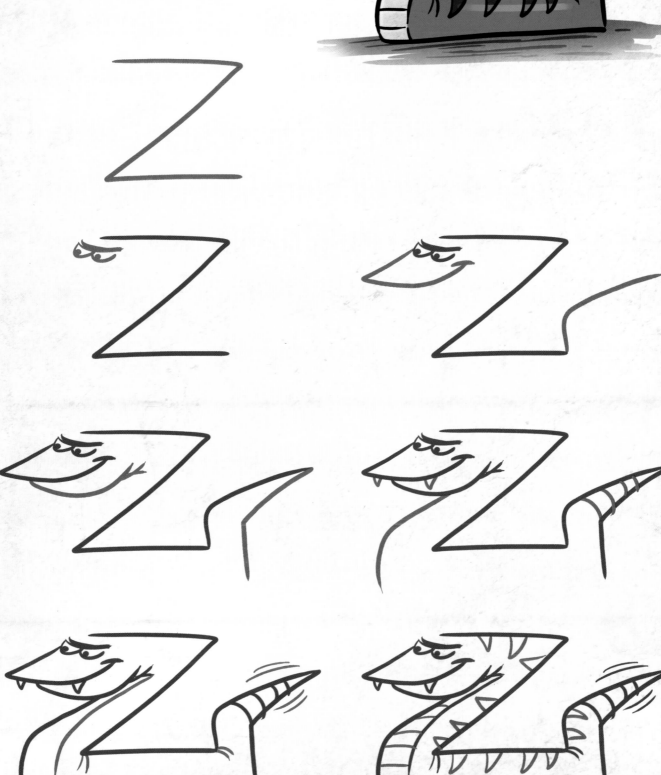

Steve Harpster lives in Cincinnati, Ohio with his lovely wife, cute little boy, and two big slobbering dogs. This is the fifth book published by his company, Harptoons Publishing.

HARPTOONS.COM

- **Watch how-to-draw videos**
- **Download drawing, coloring, and activity pages**
- **Sign your school up for a free, live online visit with Steve Harpster**
- **Free lesson plans for the classroom**

Other books by Harptoons Publishing

- Drawing Animals With Numbers
- Drawing Monsters With Letters
- Drawing Sea Animals With Numbers
- Drawing Really Cute Baby Animals With Lowercase Letters

Check out the brand new app for iPad and iPhone

DRAWING ANIMALS WITH NUMBERS The App

- Animated Drawing Steps
- Simple Navigation
- Drawing Tips Video
- Turn numbers 1-20 into cartoon animals

HARPTOONS
PUBLISHING

www.harptoons.com